CW01466414

THE
WISDOM
OF
ALOHARIN

THE
WISDOM
OF
ALOHARIN

PAUL ISHERWOOD

Contents

1

The Doorway

SOPHIA PRESSED HER FOREHEAD against the cool glass of the café window, watching another perfectly ordinary Tuesday pass by. At twenty-three, she still felt like she didn't know what to do with her life.

What am I even doing? The question came often, some days louder than others. Everyone else seemed to have it figured out: careers they were happy in, relationships that mattered, some clear sense of direction. But Sophia was drifting, with no idea what she was meant to do.

Everyone said she just needed to be practical. Just pick something stable and build from there. But stable felt like a death sentence. The idea of spending forty years in some random office job, counting down to weekends, made her chest tighten with panic.

I want to enjoy what I do, she thought fiercely. *Is that too much to ask?*

And it wasn't just about work. When she looked around at couples holding hands, laughing together, she felt that familiar pang of longing. Would finding someone special fill this hollow ache inside her? Would finding love make everything fall into place, or was she just being naive?

I just want to be happy, she thought again. The question felt at once urgent and impossible. She'd tried the usual things: hobbies, going out, even meditation apps, but nothing seemed to touch that deeper yearning for... what exactly? She couldn't even name it.

Everyone talked about being successful, but how could she achieve something she couldn't define? How could she win a game when she didn't know the rules?

She had always carried a quiet ache, a tugging sense that life was meant to be more than a string of ordinary days. However many self-help books she devoured, however many careers she considered, something always felt just out of reach. An unnamed longing. A sense of absence that no one else seemed to notice.

She longed for her life to feel special, for her days to hold purpose and meaning. But reality moved in familiar, well-worn patterns, and any glimmer of magic she found lived only between the covers of books.

Sophia sighed and gathered her things. At least there was one place where these questions faded, where the world felt full of possibility instead of limitation.

It was in bookshops that she felt most alive, wandering hushed aisles as though in a temple, the scent of old paper and ink like incense. The shelves whispered of other worlds, other lives, lives where people discovered their destinies, found their soulmates, became the heroes of their own stories. Her favourites were fantasy stories of magic and wonder, tales that cracked open the mundane and let the marvellous seep through.

She stepped out into the grey afternoon and made her way towards her favourite bookshop, her thoughts still circling in the same unhelpful loop.

Maybe that's my problem, she thought, walking towards her sanctuary. *I'm still clinging to some childish dream – expecting life to be something it isn't.*

The little bookshop she loved most stood tucked along a cobbled lane. As she reached the old streetlamp outside the shop, she always felt as though she had reached her own little piece of Narnia, a place where anything might be possible.

The shop's Victorian glass panes and beautifully carved oak door gave it the air of something timeless. At the centre of the door was a small glass pane in the most luminous shades of blue – a detail so lovely it made her pause each time she passed through, wondering if beauty this simple could be a sign that there was more magic in the world than she'd been allowing herself to believe.

Inside, the world seemed to exhale. Light pooled gently across the floor, the scent of books hung like something sacred in the air, and the old wooden floorboards creaked softly beneath her feet.

She made her way to her usual spot by the window to do her favourite thing: settle in with a hot chocolate and a few books pulled from the shelves. But today, even this couldn't quiet her restless thoughts.

She closed the book and let her gaze wander across the shop's shadowed corners, filled with stories of people who'd found their purpose, their love, their adventures.

Will I ever find what I am looking for?

As her gaze drifted to the back of the shop, something caught her eye, a flicker of light reflected off the books in a strangely captivating way. It shimmered and shifted, as if dancing across the spines with quiet intention. She watched, entranced. Then, almost without realising, she rose from her chair, drawn toward the shelves bathed in that soft, elusive light.

In the shadowed back corner, Sophia's eyes were drawn to the spine of a book she had never seen before. Its title shimmered faintly in the light, like a whisper:

The Wisdom of Aloharin

She froze, as if seeing something both familiar and yet out of place. There was something about the title, the way it was written, the way it seemed to glow in the light.

She reached up, fingers curling around the spine, and as she pulled the book gently towards herself, a soft click echoed behind the wood.

Sophia drew back, startled, as the tall bookcase gave a slow, creaking shudder and slid backwards, revealing a golden light that spilled softly through the widening gap.

She looked around, but there was no sign of anyone else in the shop.

Her heart was racing and yet in the golden light, a quiet certainty rose within her.

This is where you are meant to go.

She took a tentative step forward into a room radiant with light. It took a moment for her eyes to adjust. Then Sophia began to notice bright specks of colour amidst bright white and gold.

As everything came into focus, the sight that met her eyes stole her breath away. It was as though she had wandered into a dream made real. The room was circular, with bookshelves lining the walls from floor to ceiling. Many of the books sparkled like treasure, their spines gleaming in hues of sapphire, emerald, and gold.

High above, a glass-domed ceiling caught the sunlight and scattered golden beams that danced across the room. Everywhere she looked, soft gold accents shimmered across the books, along the ornate mouldings and across the white marble floor.

Underfoot, the polished marble was inlaid with a golden pattern at its centre, a design that spiralled outward like a labyrinth, ancient and mysterious. As Sophia made her way further into this wonderful room, her eyes traced its delicate paths. Then her gaze lifted again, and she noticed something glinting. Inlaid into the spines of certain books were small blue gemstones, vivid and bright.

At the heart of the room stood a table and chair, simple, elegant, and inviting. And to one side, a velvet sofa in deep green, edged in gold, seemed to beckon her nearer.

She stood motionless, wonder swelling in her chest. She felt, with quiet certainty, that she had crossed not only into something magical, but into the very heart of her own longing. A place impossibly beautiful, and yet, somehow, it felt like home.

Slowly, as if afraid to break the spell, she drifted toward the centre of the room, her gaze drawn upward to the radiant dome. Behind her, the door clicked gently shut, and almost at once, a second door across the chamber creaked open.

She stood frozen, caught between one door and the next. Then, drawn by something unseen, she moved towards the open doorway.

She stepped forward and gently pushed the door open. It swung outward, and as the room began to reveal itself, she caught her breath.

2

The Elders of Aloharin

BEYOND LAY A VAST library, soaring like a cathedral. Marble pillars stretched into shadowed heights. Endless shelves lined the walls. Light streamed through towering windows, turning the air to gold. People wandered the aisles, their footsteps soft on the stone, but now they began to stop and turn, staring at Sophia as if she had stepped from another world. And in truth, she had.

She blinked, feeling slightly dazed. Slowly, her feet began to move. Her eyes lifted to take in the immense ceiling above her and the towering stone columns that framed the space like a dream. Around her, people continued to stare, their eyes full of questions. She tried to smile and nod politely as she passed, aware of the many eyes upon her. And yet, strangely, she didn't feel afraid or exposed. It was as though something unseen held her in safety, a quiet feeling of protection surrounding her.

She moved toward a pair of immense wooden doors at the far end. One stood slightly ajar, and through it, she glimpsed a flash of brilliant blue sky.

Then a low, reverent voice came from behind her, breaking through the spell she had been under. She turned to see who had spoken, and found an older woman standing before her, regal and radiant in flowing robes of deep blue and gold. Her silver hair was gathered neatly at her nape, and her face held a gentle kindness.

Her gaze lingered on Sophia's face, especially her eyes, and a flicker of recognition passed across her expression, as though something long silent within her had just awakened.

'Saphira,' the woman whispered, her voice trembling. 'Is it truly you? Just as it was written... bringing light and wisdom? You have come at last?'

Sophia just looked at the woman, trying to make sense of her words, but they didn't. None of it did. She opened her mouth to speak, to explain that her name was Sophia, not Saphira, but the words wouldn't come. They hovered on her lips, unspoken, as though some deeper part of herself already understood.

The woman stepped closer. There was reverence in her eyes and something soft that put Sophia's heart gently at ease. Then, with great tenderness, she reached out and took Sophia's arm.

'Oh, my dear,' she said, her voice warm and lilting. 'This must be quite something to take in. I imagine you've been on quite the journey.'

Sophia nodded, still too stunned to form a proper answer. Her gaze swept again across the magnificent marble floor, the shelves of glowing books and the golden sunlight pouring through high windows.

'Where are we?' she whispered.

The woman smiled, her eyes twinkling with quiet delight as she answered.

'You, dear one, are in Aloharin.'

She paused for a moment, then added gently, 'I'm sure you have so many questions. I think now would be the perfect time for a little sit-down and a good old-fashioned cup of Aloharian tea. And you can ask as many questions as you would like.'

Sophia nodded again, grateful for the kindness and calm in her voice.

'Come,' the woman said, guiding her gently across the library floor. 'We'll go this way.'

They walked together toward a tall door carved from pale wood and inscribed in gold with the words: Elders' Terrace.

The woman opened the door, and they stepped out onto the most beautiful terrace Sophia had ever seen.

She stood still for a moment and her mouth fell open in awe.

Spread out before them was the city of Aloharin. Its rooftops of turquoise blue and soft orange were dotted with domes and towers, glinting in the sunlight like gems. The sky above was the clearest blue she had ever seen, and just beyond the city's edge, she could make out the gentle rise and fall of the ocean's waves, shimmering in the distance.

The terrace itself was shaded by flowering vines that trailed from carved stone columns. Colourful cushions lined elegant benches and chairs. It felt both grand and peaceful. This terrace was so idyllic and beautiful, Sophia felt that it must belong to someone important, perhaps royalty. Then she remembered the sign on the door and wondered who these Elders truly were.

'Please,' the woman said, gesturing to a chair by a long, glass-topped table. 'Sit.'

As they settled, a teenage girl nearby straightened some cushions and tidied another table.

The older woman turned to her with a gentle smile. 'Elfira, dear, would you bring us some tea? And ask Elder Alfonso to come. Tell him we have a very special guest.'

Sophia turned again to take in the sweeping panorama, unaware that the older woman was watching her with just as much wonder.

The woman's name was Eleonora, chief librarian of Aloharin and the long-trusted keeper of the prophecy. It was a long-guarded belief that someone would one day come to reveal the ancient wisdom once more. She had been its student and later its guardian, its voice. And now, before her, stood the one it had promised.

Just as Eleonora was about to speak, the door behind them opened.

A tall, striking man entered, his powder-blue robes flowing softly as he stepped into the light. Though older, there was strength in his bearing and a quiet grace in the way he moved. His silver hair was pulled back into an elegant ponytail, his beard gleaming, and his eyes bright with intelligence and warmth.

He paused at the threshold and smiled. 'Who is this special guest?'

But when he saw Sophia, her clothes clearly not of this world and those clear, searching blue eyes, his smile faded. Something shifted in his expression. The quiet magnitude of the moment settled between them like a hush.

Eleonora met his gaze, her eyes almost overflowing with emotion. She gave the smallest nod, as if to say, It's her.

And Alfonso, who had seen many things in his lifetime, from miracles to mysteries and magic, stood perfectly still.

Sophia looked up, unsure and yet with a flicker of knowing, as if they had met long ago in some place beyond memory.

Then Alfonso stepped forward with grace and humility, recovering his composure with a gentle smile.

'I am Alfonso,' he said kindly. 'And who are you, my dear?'

Sophia opened her mouth, still uncertain. But before she could answer, Eleonora gently placed her hand over hers.

'This,' she said softly, 'is Saphira.'

And though it startled Sophia to hear it spoken again, some part of her accepted the name as if it had always belonged to her.

They sat together for a long while on the sun-dappled terrace, where tea was brought, sweet fruit was laid out on delicate plates, and birds sang in the vines overhead. In the warm, quiet stillness, Eleonora and Alfonso began to speak.

They told her of the prophecy: of a time when the Chamber of Wisdom, sealed for generations, would open once more. Of books that held the great truths of life, love, joy, and creation – books that could only be read by the one who was destined to come. Of a task not of rule or command, but of remembrance – to learn, to live, and to carry that wisdom back into the hearts of the people.

They spoke with awe and quiet gratitude, thankful that she had come and that the long waiting was over.

Through that conversation, and the many questions she asked, Sophia began to understand what had truly happened. She had not simply discovered a hidden room; she had stepped into a living prophecy, one whispered in old songs and kept alive by the oldest of the elders. It was said that a prophet named Saphira would one day return to reveal the forgotten wisdom of Aloharin.

From the moment she arrived, Sophia was no longer called by her old name. To the people of Aloharin, she was and always would be Saphira.

3

The Prophet of Aloharin

THE MORNING AFTER HER arrival, a new chapter quietly began.

At dawn, Eleonora led her through the golden hush of the city towards the Chamber of Wisdom. The streets were still, bathed in amber light. Sophia walked beside her in silence, aware that she would need to grow into the name the people had given her.

The night before, Eleonora had explained this part of the prophecy. It was said that the Chamber would recognise Saphira and open itself to her, and to her alone. From that day forward, she would have access to its great wisdom. She could return whenever she desired, and when the time felt right, she would share what she learned. Not all at once. Never by obligation. But in her own way and at her own pace.

As they made their way through the Grand Library, Saphira paused to take in its beauty, just as she had the day before. She walked slowly, her gaze lifting in quiet admiration.

Then, at last, she found herself standing before the great door to the chamber, tall and ancient, carved from pale wood streaked with threads of gold. Symbols and markings had been etched into its surface long ago, their meaning forgotten, though some whispered they were blessings from the first keepers of the wisdom.

Inlaid at eye level was a single sapphire-coloured stone, smooth as glass. As her eyes met its surface, it shimmered faintly, and the door clicked softly open, as though the chamber itself had recognised her. As though it had been waiting.

That same afternoon, Eleonora took her to a sunlit studio on the edge of the city, where silken fabrics hung like waterfalls and the air was scented with jasmine. There, she met Arena, a warm-hearted woman with silvery hair braided with gold thread. She had long created garments for the elders, famed for weaving beauty into every stitch. But upon meeting Saphira, she felt a reverence that stirred from somewhere deeper than tradition.

'You must be Saphira,' Arena said, her smile as gentle as the morning light. 'Eleonora told me you'd be coming and I've been so looking forward to meet you'

Over the following days, Arena created a collection of garments in the traditional Aloharin style: flowing robes and fine clothing made from the finest fabrics, each one crafted with quiet elegance and care.

The wardrobe included pieces for every occasion, all bearing Saphira's name embroidered in either gleaming gold or brilliant blue silk.

In the days that followed, two quiet guardians were assigned to her: Marek and Petrin, kind-faced protectors who watched over her from a respectful distance. Marek, the elder of the two, carried himself with calm solemnity, his silver-streaked hair always neatly bound. Petrin, younger but no less devoted, had a gentler gaze and a quiet attentiveness that never faltered.

They never interfered, never spoke unless spoken to, but their presence was constant. Whether Saphira studied at the top of the Grand Library steps or wandered to Aloha Shores with a scroll in hand, they were near. Silent. Steady. Honouring the sacred work unfolding in her care, not just as guards, but as witnesses to something greater than themselves.

She became known throughout Aloharin as the prophet: a gentle guide, a teacher of joy and a whisperer of truth. Day by day, she immersed herself in the glowing books of the Chamber, learning secrets that seemed to light her from within. No one but Saphira could enter the Chamber of Wisdom, and each day she emerged with new insights, pearls of light to offer a waiting world.

People would often gather at the foot of the steps of the Grand Library, sometimes for hours, hoping to glimpse her, to hear a few words that might ease a burden or brighten a path.

And Saphira gave gladly. She loved her days of study and sharing. She loved Aloharin, a place of breathtaking beauty, where she had grown to feel a deep belonging. But in her heart, she always knew: her time here was not forever. From the beginning, she had felt the quiet truth, that the door she had stepped through would one day open again, calling her back to the world she had left behind.

This part of the prophecy was no secret. The people of Aloharin had always known the time of Saphira would one day come to an end. And that day had come.

It had been seven years since that first miraculous day.

Seven years since Sophia had crossed the threshold into Aloharin and become part of its legend.

She had arrived a stranger, unknown and unsure.

And in time she had become one of the most cherished figures in their history.

But now, that chapter was drawing to a close.

Standing on the marble steps at the foot of the Grand Library, Saphira gazed out over the sunlit square, where hundreds had gathered. The evening light painted the buildings gold and the air shimmered with soft voices, hushed and hopeful. The word had travelled fast: this was Saphira's last day in Aloharin.

Among the crowd gathered at the foot of the steps, the elders waited in quiet stillness, watchful and open-hearted. Eleonora and Alfonso were side by side, their expressions full of quiet reverence. They had shared countless evenings with Saphira: warm meals, laughter, and long conversations beneath the flowering vines of the Elders' Terrace. They had offered their stories, and listened in wonder as she told hers. Bonds had formed not only through wisdom, but through kindness, humour, and the gentle rhythm of shared days.

And beside them was Elfira. No longer the bright-eyed apprentice she had once been, but a young woman full of grace and quiet strength. Over the years, she and Saphira had become like sisters. They had shared laughter, secrets, layful mischief and moments of quiet truth. Elfira had been a breath of fresh air in Saphira's mission to study and serve the people of Aloharin. In return, she had absorbed much of Saphira's insight and light. So close had they become that some said they had even begun to resemble each other.

Now, as Saphira prepared to leave, Elfira looked as though her heart might break. Eleonora and Alfonso stood close beside her, their arms gently around her shoulders, offering what comfort they could, but it was clear she struggled to be consoled.

In the weeks before, the elders had spoken often of what might unfold.

'We must be ready,' one had said. 'If she chooses to speak, we must be able to carry her words forward.'

And so they had asked their finest scribe to be present on this final day, a quiet elder named Thalen, known for his clarity of heart and grace with words.

He waited now, scroll in hand, ink prepared, ready to capture the light of whatever might be shared. Not for himself, but for the people of Aloharin and for generations yet to come.

To ensure no word would be lost, Thalen brought his sharp-eyed apprentice Lira, who stood ready with parchment and ink, ready to catch each phrase with quiet precision.

At the base of the steps, a murmur rose, a single plea, picked up and carried by the crowd:

'Saphira, before you leave us – share your wisdom once more, so we may carry it in our hearts when you are gone!'

Saphira closed her eyes for a moment, breathing in the golden light, feeling the ache of parting rise and swell inside her.

She felt a deep love for them all: for the people of Aloharin and for those dearest to her. For Alfonso, with his quiet wisdom and humour. For Eleonora, whose presence had been like a guiding lamp from the very beginning.

And for Elfira, sweet, brilliant Elfira, who now stood with tear-filled eyes, barely holding herself together. As Saphira looked at her, she felt her own tears rising, the weight of their bond pressing softly against her chest. She longed to go to her, to gather her close one last time. But instead, she drew in a breath and steadied herself.

She was here now as their prophet. This moment was not for sorrow, but for offering.

And yet, beneath the sadness, there was peace. A deep, quiet knowing that all was well, that this, too, was part of the journey.

She opened her eyes and smiled, a soft, radiant smile full of love. She lifted her hands in blessing, her cloak catching the last light of the setting sun, her presence a quiet beacon.

And then she stepped forward, her voice ready to weave its final gift.

4

What Is the Purpose of Life?

FROM THE CROWD, A young woman stepped forward, her hands resting gently on the curve of her belly. Her eyes shone with wonder and a trace of uncertainty.

She lifted her voice and asked,
'Saphira, before you leave us... tell me. Why do we come into this world? What is the purpose of this life?'

Saphira met her gaze with warmth and tenderness.
For a moment, she was silent, her hand resting gently over her heart. Then she began.

'This is one of the great questions of the soul.

Especially in difficult moments, we wonder: why would we choose to come here at all?

To begin to understand, we must first remember:

You are more than this body.

You are part of something eternal.

You are part of the divine.

And before you were born, from beyond this world, you chose to come.

When you remember this, the answer begins to unfold.

You came not to struggle.

Not to prove anything.

Not to be tested.

You can because you longed to taste the wonder of it.

You came to feel joy.

To walk among beauty.

To discover what it means to love and be loved.

To create, to explore, to grow,

and to know the deep, steady satisfaction of living in harmony with your heart.

Everything you dream of, every hope, every desire, is not for the thing itself,

but for how you believe it will make you feel.

And the feeling you are seeking, underneath it all, is joy.

This is the compass of life.

This is the golden thread that runs through it all.

And when you begin to believe that this joy is not some trivial thing,

but your purpose, everything begins to change.

We must not make light of this.

To live a life of joy, of upliftment and peace, is no small thing.

Do not mistake success for something found only in wealth or winning.

It is fine to wish for those things, of course. But the true prize, the real measure, is how you feel within your life.

You can succeed in the quietest of days,

not by doing something extraordinary,

but simply by how you feel.

Even the smallest moment,

a laugh, a calm breath or a shared smile, can be a triumph.

For joy is not something small.

It is what we came for.

And there is a power beyond the physical,

a wisdom that walks beside you always,

helping you to live the life you came here to live.

And now, as you welcome new life into this world,
this wisdom is made visible again.

For when your child arrives,
they will remind you of everything you've forgotten.
You'll see it in the way they reach for joy in every moment.
How they play, how they giggle, how they turn the ordinary into delight.

You'll notice they are never far from wonder.
They are rarely distracted by worry.
They are here. Present. Alive.
Seeing the world with clear, astonished eyes.

And in watching them,
you will remember what it is to live with lightness.
To seek what feels good.
To follow curiosity.
To laugh for no reason.
To trust the goodness of life.

And when you remember,

you will feel more joy in your own life.

You will walk together, hand in hand,

not just as mother and child,

but as companions on a great and beautiful adventure.

The woman's eyes shimmered as Saphira's words settled into her heart. She placed both hands gently over her belly, and for a moment, she simply breathed.

A feeling rose within her, warm, steady and bright. It was as if some ancient part of her had finally remembered life was unfolding as it should, and was destined to be more beautiful than she had ever imagined.

5

Who Am I Meant to Become?

As Saphira's words settled over the gathering, many sat quietly, the idea of joy as purpose gently turning over in their minds.

A young dreamer, her eyes wide with wonder, stepped forward.

'If joy is the reason we came, then... how does this help me know who I'm meant to become?' she asked gently.

And Saphira replied:

'You are not here to become someone else.
You are here to become more of yourself.
You were born already whole:
already carrying the seeds of your dreams,
already aligned with the song your soul longs to sing.

Becoming is not about chasing a fixed destiny,
nor meeting some outside expectation.
It is about unfolding, moment by moment,
into the fullest, brightest version of the being you
already are.

The signs are always within you:
the things that light you up,
the moments that fill you with joy,
the dreams that stir your heart
even when no one else understands them.

Trust what calls you.
Follow the path that feels alive under your feet.

You do not need to force it,
nor figure it all out at once.

Your becoming is a journey, not a race.
And along the way,
tell yourself, again and again,
even if you long for more,
and even when there are things you wish to change,
that you are already enough,
already worthy.'

The young dreamer stood still for a while, letting the words settle gently inside her. She felt lighter, as if something quietly wonderful had shifted. And though she didn't yet have all the answers, she could imagine what it might feel like to follow her heart and begin believing in herself.

6

Does Money Bring Happiness?

Saphira's words lingered in the air, leaving a thoughtful hush among all those who listened.

Then a merchant stepped forward, older and wearier, his hands clasped tightly and worry etched into his brow.

'Saphira,' he said, 'I hear what you say about joy being our purpose, and to trust what calls us... but I've done what I thought were the "right" things. I've earned. I've saved. And still... I don't feel peace.

Why hasn't money brought me happiness?'

Saphira turned to him, her eyes soft with understanding.

'What you truly long for is not money,
but the feeling you hoped it would bring.

You want to feel safe.
Free.
At ease in your life.
Able to rest without fear
and wake with joy in your chest.

That longing is not wrong.
But hear me:
money, by itself, cannot bring happiness.
Not lasting happiness.
Not peace.

It can open doors.

It can offer comfort.
But if your mind is tuned to fear,
no amount will ever feel like enough.

Peace does not come from how much you have.

Rich or poor may know deep joy,
or either may live in fear.
What makes the difference
is not what they hold,
but what they fear and believe.

When you begin to shift your attention
from what's missing
to what's already here,
you begin to feel rich inside,
and the world begins to reflect that richness back to
you.

This does not mean you must stop wanting more.
Desire is natural.

It is life calling you forward.

Let it rise.

But let it rise from love, not lack.

Meanwhile, look around.

Look within.

Your breath.

Your body.

The light through the window.

The taste of food.

The voice of someone who loves you.

These are not small things.

They are treasures.

And when you begin to feel wealthy within,
you create the space for more wealth, of all kinds,
to flow towards you.

So yes, earn. Grow. Give.

Let money come.

But don't wait for it to bring happiness.

That happiness can begin now.

Ask not, "Will money make me happy?"

but rather, "How can I find peace and happiness today?"

For then you will have discovered

the wealth that the world cannot take away.'

The merchant stood silently, his eyes lowered, as if seeing something within himself for the first time. A quiet stillness came over him, not from answers alone, but from the feeling that he had just received something truly rich: the truth his heart had been waiting for.

7

What is Success?

Such wisdom about money and desire had stirred something in the crowd. But now, a hush settled over them, as if they were quietly anticipating the next question.

Then a young scholar raised his hand, a leather satchel of books slung over his shoulder, his eyes bright with ambition, yet full of questions.

He asked, 'Saphira, I want to be successful... but I realise, after listening to your words, I'm not even sure I know what it means.'

Saphira turned to him, smiling gently, as if she recognised the longing in his heart.

'Success is not measured by how high you climb,
nor by how much applause you gather,
nor by how many trophies line your shelves.

Success is measured by how fully you live,
how deeply you feel,
how often you touch joy in your days.

You may win the world and yet feel hollow.
You may lose a race and yet feel whole.

The world will offer you many definitions of success:
wealth, fame, achievement, mastery.
But none of these can bring you peace

if you lose yourself in the process.

True success is the art of tending to your own spirit:
of following the path that lights you up,
of waking each morning eager for the day,
and resting each night with a quiet, satisfied heart.

You succeed not when you prove yourself,
but when you are true to yourself.
You succeed not when you earn love,
but when you let love flow through you freely.

So, young seeker,
pursue what calls you.
But remember:
the feeling is the prize,
and the joy you experience on your journey
is the true measure of success.'

The scholar felt the truth of Saphira's words settling warmly inside him, as if success had just taken on a whole new shape, one that felt far more true.

He smiled, quietly proud to have spoken, and to have been part of this historic gathering.

8

Is Joy Really in the Journey?

WHEN A STILLNESS SETTLED over the gathering once again, a traveller stepped forward, dust on his boots, a map curled in his hand and weariness etched across his face.

He looked at Saphira thoughtfully and said,

'Saphira, you spoke of success being found in the journey itself.

But what if I don't feel the joy everyone talks about?

What if I just want to get where I'm going?'

Saphira turned to him, her eyes full of compassion,

as if she understood the ache of striving without peace.

And she replied:

'What you are truly longing for
is never the destination itself.
It is the feeling you believe the destination will bring.

You think:
When I arrive, I will be happy.
When I succeed, I will feel whole.
When I achieve this dream, I will be at peace.

'But hear this.'
She looked slowly around at those gathered.
'You are always on a journey.
You are only ever passing through destinations,
briefly,
before you set your eyes on the next horizon.

If you wait for joy only at the finish line,
you will miss the thousands of joys
that walk beside you every day.

The purpose of life
is not to get it all done,
but to discover how to feel good as you go.

When you find joy in the step you are taking now,
you unlock the secret:
you are already receiving
what you thought was waiting at the end.

So lift your eyes.
Let the road delight you.
Let the little moments fill your cup.

Because the truth is,
there will always be another journey,
another dream,
another becoming.

Joy is not a prize at the end.

It is the golden thread woven through it all.'

The traveller listened intently, hanging on every word. As the truth of Saphira's words settled within him, his shoulders eased and the tightness in his brow began to soften. Saphira's gentle smile met his eyes, and he found himself smiling back, not with certainty, but with a quiet sense of peace that, somehow, he was already on the right path.

9

Where Do I Belong?

THE CROWD HAD TAKEN in Saphira's words with quiet reverence, just as the traveller had. A soft ripple of clapping rose, accompanied by murmurs of appreciation. But as a small boy stepped forward from the edge of the gathering, the sound began to fade. One by one, people hushed each other, and a gentle stillness settled once more.

He asked,
'Saphira... I don't have parents or grandparents. Sometimes I wonder... am I unwanted?

Where do I belong?'

Saphira knelt before him, her eyes soft with understanding,
and replied:

'You, dear one, belong to a love
far greater than you can yet see.

The love of parents is eternal.
Even when they are no longer here,
even when you cannot touch them or hear their voices,
their love remains.
It follows you,
holds you,
guides you.

And when others step in,
a kind teacher, a caring friend, a guardian or guide,
they are not second-best.

They are life's way of reminding you
that you are never alone.

You belong not because someone claims you.
You belong because you are a child of life itself.

You are not unwanted.
You are not forgotten.
You are a soul made of light,
and love has been reaching for you
from the moment you arrived.

This love is deeper than time or memory.
It lives within you,
and it goes with you always.'

Saphira looked up from the boy,
then slowly lifted her gaze to the faces around her.
Her voice, still gentle, now carried a quiet strength.

'And this message is not only for the child before me,

but for every soul who has ever wondered:
Do I matter?
Do I belong?
Am I truly loved?

Yes, you do.
Yes, you are.
Yes, you always have been.

Every kindness you receive,
every hand that holds yours,
every bit of love you give or receive
is part of that great belonging.

And if your parents are still living but seem distant
or cold,
know this:
they are not broken.
They are simply out of touch with the love that lives
within them.
One day, that love will awaken,

in this life or beyond,
and they will remember who they truly are.

So hold your head high.
Let your light shine without shrinking.
You are part of the great family of life,
and the world is better
because you are here.'

The boy gazed at her with wide, shining eyes. Then, with a sudden bright smile, he ran forward and threw his arms around her.

Soft laughter rippled through the crowd, followed by a wave of warm applause. Some reached for each other's hands. Others turned and whispered in awe, amazed by the wonder of what they had just heard and what they had felt.

10

What Is Love?

The boy slowly released Saphira and made his way back to his place, his face still glowing with the light of her words. The applause softened into silence, but the feeling of connection lingered. And from that stillness, something else began to stir.

From among the crowd, a young couple stepped forward. Their hands were loosely entwined, their expressions uncertain. It felt almost impossible to speak after such a tender moment, after the applause,

the tears, the silence. And yet, something in them still
needed to ask.

They stood quietly for a moment. Then one of them
looked up and said,

'Saphira, what is love?

It can be so confusing.

One day it feels amazing, the next it feels awful.

What is love really meant to be?'

Saphira looked at them gently,

as if she saw not only their question,

but the quiet ache beneath it.

'Yes, love can feel confusing.

It can lift you higher than anything,

and it can hurt in ways nothing else does.

But that pain doesn't come from love itself,

it comes from forgetting where love truly begins.

Love is not something you find.

It is something you remember.

Love is the natural light of your being.
It is the essence of who you are
before fear, before judgement,
before the world taught you to measure your worth.

You often search for love in others,
hoping someone will fill what feels missing within
you.
But the most important love you will ever find
is the love you give to yourself.

Not because others cannot be trusted,
but because no one else can live inside your heart.
No one else can speak to you in every moment,
soothing your worries,
celebrating your joy,
reminding you that you are enough.

When you love yourself,

you do not become selfish.
You become whole.

You stop needing others to prove your worth.
You stop fearing their distance,
or clinging to their praise.

And from that place of wholeness,
you can love others more freely,
not to get something,
but to share something.

Love given from fullness is peace.
Love given from emptiness becomes a plea.

So begin with yourself.
Hold yourself as gently as you long to be held.
See yourself through the eyes of the divine:
always worthy,
always growing,
always loved.

And then,
when you look at another,
you will see the divine in them too.

True love is not possession.
It is recognition.
It is remembering that both of you
are expressions of the same sacred light.

Let your love be kind.
Let it be spacious.
Let it leave room for both of you to grow.

And above all,
let it begin within.

For the love you long for
is already within you,
waiting to be discovered,
and gently nurtured.'

The couple turned to one another, and in that moment, a quiet knowing passed between them. Not the solving of every question, but the soft recognition of something true.

They laughed, then embraced. And the crowd, touched once more, broke into gentle applause, grateful for another luminous moment, and for the blessing of being part of this extraordinary evening.

11

Healing a Broken Heart

THE TENDER MOMENT BETWEEN the young couple had passed, but something of it lingered in the air. There was a soft joy among the gathering, the kind that comes from being reminded of love. Yet beneath the smiles, some hearts were quietly aching, not with joy remembered, but with love lost.

Near the edge of the crowd, a young man stood with his head bowed. He had only just tasted love for the first time, and just as suddenly, it was gone. His heart ached in a way he had never known before. He wanted to ask Saphira how to feel better, how to stop hurting, but he was too shy, too afraid.

Just then, a woman stepped forward from among the people, a widow, with her daughter's hand resting gently in her own. With teary eyes, she asked her question:

'Saphira... how do we carry on when love is lost?
How do we heal a heart that's been broken?'

The young man looked up, startled. It was his question. Every word of it. And in that moment, he felt the love of which Saphira had spoken, a quiet warmth stirring in his chest, and tears began to gather in his eyes.

Saphira listened to the woman, her face full of compassion.

And before she began to speak, she let her gaze drift gently to the young man, as if to say, *These words are for you too.*

'When love ends,
your thoughts may circle the empty space it leaves behind.
You replay memories, moments,
trying to hold on, trying to understand.
And in doing so,
you keep reopening the wound.

But love was never meant to trap you in pain.
It was meant to remind you of the beauty
you are capable of feeling.
And that beauty is still alive within you now.

It may not feel that way today.
That's all right.
You are allowed to grieve.
But even in grief,

you are not powerless.

You have the quiet strength
to shift your gaze – just a little.
To reach for a thought that feels softer.
To notice the way the sky holds light,
or the way a stranger's smile warms your heart for no
reason at all.

Love doesn't live only in one person.
It lives in you.
And when your heart begins to open again,
you will see love everywhere.
In kindness shared,
in beauty noticed,
in life itself.

Do not wait for love to find you again.
Become it.

Share your kindness freely.

Speak gently.
Bring joy to others.
And in doing so,
you will bring joy to yourself.

Every time you offer warmth to another soul,
you give a piece of that warmth to your own heart.
And slowly, the pain loosens.
Slowly, your heart mends.'

The young man looked up,
his face streaked with tears.
But there was light in his eyes now.
A flicker of something returning.

The widow brought her daughter's hand to her
chest,
as if to hold the moment still within her.
She no longer felt quite so alone.

A hush had settled over the gathering once again,

perhaps of hearts quietly mending,

each one holding the tender knowledge

that healing was possible,

and love would always return.

12

Peace of Mind

Saphira's words had comforted many. Some now sat in quiet contentment, grateful to have heard what their hearts had long needed. But not every question had yet been answered.

From within the crowd, a young girl stepped forward, still wearing her Aloharin school uniform. She held her father's hand tightly, gently pulling him with her.

The man looked uncomfortable in the silence, his clothes dusty and worn from labour, his face lined with exhaustion.

The girl glanced up at him, then turned to Saphira. She said softly,

'My father works so hard.

He's always helping others.

He goes to work early and comes back late,

and still finds time to cook, or fix things, or help me with my schoolwork.

But... he always looks tired.

And sometimes he gets angry, even when he doesn't mean to.

I know he's doing his best.

I just hoped maybe your words could help him.'

The father was both surprised and moved by his daughter's words. He ran a hand over his tired face, but said nothing.

Saphira regarded them both with quiet compassion. She nodded slowly, as if understanding every unspoken burden behind the girl's words. Then, looking directly at the father, she said:

'You are not alone in your struggle.
So many believe that in order to support those we love,
we must work harder, push further,
use every moment to fix, plan and provide.

And so, day by day,
they begin to sacrifice themselves.
Their rest, their joy, their dreams.

But when you give all of yourself away,
you become stretched thin,
and the love you wish to offer becomes difficult to find.
You carry more stress,
and sometimes, without meaning to,

you hurt the very ones you care for most.

In time, your body speaks.
The constant giving begins to wear you down.
Exhaustion settles in,
and if left unheard,
it can grow into illness.
And suddenly,
you are the one who needs care.

So let me tell you something that many forget:
The best way to help those you love
is to include yourself in the love that you give,
and not as an afterthought, but as a priority.

When you give yourself even a little peace of mind,
you reconnect with your strength.
You become clearer, calmer, healthier.

And from that place,
you will be far more capable

to offer the help and presence others truly need.

Even more,
you will become an example.
And that is the greatest gift you can give.

So start not by doing more,
but by pausing.
By finding even a small moment
to meet yourself in stillness.'

She paused, letting her words settle across the gathering.

Then she returned her gaze to the girl.

'And these words are for you too,' she said with a loving smile.

The girl looked up at Saphira, her eyes wide as if to say, *Who, me?*

Saphira nodded gently.

'Yes... because even in your own young heart,
there can be a weight no one else sees.
You carry expectations,
questions about who you should be,
fears of not being enough,
and worries you never speak aloud.

In trying to keep up, to do well, to be liked,
you can lose touch with your own voice.
That quiet voice inside
that knows what you truly need.

When you give yourself even a little peace of mind,
you reconnect with your strength.
You hear your intuition again.'

Saphira paused once more and looked at the father,
then up at the crowd again,
as if to make sure everyone knew this message was for
them.

Then she said:

'Before the world rushes in,
before the noise of the day begins,
give yourself one gentle gift.

A few quiet minutes that belong only to you.
No need to think, or plan, or solve.
No pressure to be anything at all.
A moment of peace,
and perhaps even a quiet kind of bliss.

Sit with your eyes closed,
and let your thoughts drift like leaves on water.
Don't chase them.
Don't wrestle them.
Just let them pass.

If it helps, listen to the sound of the ocean,
or the soft crackle of a fire.

Something steady. Something soothing.
Like the rhythm of your own breath.

Even two minutes like this
can open a door to peace.

And as you return to this quiet space each morning,
you will begin to feel it calling you.
Not as a duty,
but as a blessing.

And you may find that two minutes becomes five.
And five becomes ten.
Because the more you taste this gift,
the more you'll want to return to it.

This is how you tune yourself
to the frequency of your own wellbeing.
This is how you open yourself
to clarity, strength and grace.

Let it become your most sacred habit.

And from this place of stillness,
you will move through your day
not with tension,
but with quiet power.

You will become more aware
of the thoughts that move through your mind.
You will begin to notice which ones bring tension,
and which ones bring relief.
And in that awareness,
you are no longer at the mercy of old patterns.
You are empowered to choose again.
To choose thoughts that feel steadier,
kinder,
more in tune with the wisdom you've heard tonight.

And so,
you will meet your life with a calm mind and steady
heart.

And the ones you love
will feel it too.'

A hush lingered after she finished speaking. The father stood still, as if something inside him had just exhaled. He smiled at his daughter and gently squeezed her hand a little tighter. He felt the truth of Saphira's words settle deep within him.

And he wasn't the only one. Others in the gathering had been listening closely, each carrying their own burdens, their own restless thoughts.

Many had not realised how busy their minds had become, how constant the noise, how far away the stillness. But now, something had shifted.

Perhaps this was the way, many of them thought. Not to chase, not to strive, but to begin with stillness. And somewhere within them, stillness had begun to return.

13

Does God Exist?

Something rare had been offered, a doorway into stillness, and many felt as though they had stepped through. Some closed their eyes. Others sat with soft smiles, held by a calm they hadn't realised they were missing.

And yet, after a while, a man stepped forward hesitantly, as though he had carried his question for many years and wasn't sure if now was the right moment to speak.

He said,

'Saphira... I've listened to you speak, and I've felt something I can't explain. It's as if the divine is in your words, in this place, in all of us. But still... this question has lived in me since I was a boy, and I would love to hear your answer.

My question is simply: does God exist?'

Saphira smiled, her face aglow with warmth, love and knowing.

She said,

'This is a most beautiful question.

And to answer it,

we must first ask another:

what does God mean to you?

For some, God is a being.

For others, a presence.

A father.

A mother.

A mystery.
A name too vast for words.

So let us speak not of images,
but of essence.

Let us speak of the presence behind the breath,
the order within the stars,
the quiet rhythm in the rising of waves.

Let us speak of the intelligence in a seed,
the harmony of planets,
the beauty that moves you.

Let us speak of love.
Because many say God is love.
And yes, we can say that.

Because love is not just a feeling.
It is a force that draws life together.
It is profound appreciation.

Love recognises that we are all connected,
our spirits entwined.
It is the power that longs to unite us,
to see the good in all,
to celebrate our differences,
to create harmony.

Love remembers the wonder and beauty of our
essence.
And so,
love is the origin,
the architect,
the endless presence from which all things come.

You do not need to prove this presence...
You feel it.

When you look at something beautiful
and sense yourself expand,
you feel it.

When you are held in grief
and something steadies you,
even as your heart breaks,
you feel it.

You feel it in joy,
in peace,
in awe,
in the quiet knowing that you are more
than bone, name, and memory.

So yes, God exists.
But we need not hold on to the name.
For while it brings comfort to some,
it can feel distant to others,
and at times even divide us.

You are not separate from the divine.
You are a strand in its tapestry,
a note in its music,
a wave in its sea.

So go in peace.
And find joy in knowing
the divine is within you,
and all around you.

The man's shoulders eased, and a quiet smile softened his face. It was the kind of smile that comes when something long questioned is finally understood.

Not because it was explained, but because it was felt.

14

What Happens When We Die?

A DEEP SILENCE FOLLOWED Saphira's answer. It was not filled with questions or even thoughts, only stillness. As if, for a moment, everyone had remembered something too vast for words.

Many believed that must be the end. For what more could be asked after speaking of God, the soul, and love itself?

But then, from the very front of the gathering, a child who had sat quietly through it all spoke.

She had been the first to arrive that day, drawn by a feeling she didn't fully understand. Something had told her to come early, to wait in that exact spot. She had followed it without question, guided by a quiet knowing, leading her forward.

She looked up at Saphira, eyes wide with quiet wonder, her whole being open, as if listening with her heart.

'Saphira,' she said gently,
'what happens when we die?
Is it the end?
Where do we go?'

Saphira looked at her with infinite tenderness, as if the child had voiced the question carried silently in every heart, but with a purity only a child could offer.

Lowering herself until they were eye to eye, Saphira placed a hand over her heart and, with the warmest smile, said softly:

'My sweet one,
thank you for asking such a beautiful question.
You are braver than you know.'

She paused, her eyes luminous with affection.

Then she rose to her full height
and let her gaze sweep across the gathering,
so that all would know
her answer was for them too.

'Death is not the end.
It is a doorway.

You are an eternal being.
This beautiful, fleeting life is but one chapter
in the great, endless story of who you are.

When you leave this world, you do not cease.
You simply change form,
just as water becomes mist,
just as day becomes night.

You return to the vast, loving realm
from whence you came.

Death is not a punishment,
nor a loss,
nor a failure.
It is a homecoming,
a reunion,
a continuation.

Those who have gone before you
are not lost.
They are near.
They are loving you,
guiding you,

walking beside you in ways unseen.

So do not fear death.
And do not waste your days
worrying over its approach.

Live now.
Love now.
Rejoice in the dance of life,
knowing that when the music changes,
it leads only to another,
even more beautiful song.'

As she spoke her final words, Saphira looked down
and met the child's eyes, bright and full of light. A
gentle smile played at the corners of the girl's mouth,
as if she had recognised a truth she had always known.

Her father had died the year before, and now, with
Saphira's words still hanging in the air, something

inside her had settled. She felt him near and knew he was the one who had guided her there.

The crowd remained still, sensing that this was the end. Saphira had spoken her final word. The atmosphere held a quiet sadness at the close of this unforgettable evening and the gentle recognition that Saphira's time in Aloharin had come to an end.

But there was joy too. A deep, steady joy that came from knowing there is no real ending. Even death is not a departure, only a turning of the page.

We are only ever separated for a moment. And even then, we are never truly far apart.

15

The Farewell

WHEN SAPHIRA SPOKE HER final words, a hush settled over the square. The sun had dropped low, and the golden light had faded into twilight. Around the gathering, the flaming braziers glowed softly along the edges of the square, their amber light flickering gently against the coming dark.

People waited in respectful stillness. No one was quite sure what would happen next.

Then the Elders stepped forward. Alfonso and Eleonora, flanked by the others, crossed the stone platform with quiet dignity.

Eleonora turned to the people, her voice steady despite the weight in her chest.

'People of Aloharin,' she said. 'The sun is setting, and the moment has come. Let us give thanks for all that has been shared, and all that has been made new.'

Her words were simple, but they opened something in the hearts of the crowd, and applause broke out . It was gentle at first, then quickly became full-hearted and overflowing.

Some placed hands over their hearts. Others stood in silence, their eyes glistening.

There were cheers and quiet smiles, laughter and soft sobs.

Love made visible in a thousand forms.

And in the centre of it all stood Saphira.

The wave of love that rose from the people moved through her like a tide and the composure she had carried all evening finally broke. Her lips parted as if to speak but no words came. Instead, tears began to spill down her face.

She looked out across the sea of faces: those she had comforted, taught, laughed with and even wept with. Her arms trembled slightly at her sides as she tried again to speak, to say thank you, but her voice caught once more.

Elfira had been standing just behind the Elders, her hands clasped tightly in front of her, as if holding herself together. She had watched Saphira throughout the evening with wide, solemn eyes, trying to be strong, trying to prepare herself for what was coming. But now, seeing Saphira falter, tears running freely down her face, something broke open inside her. The sight was too much to bear.

Before she could stop herself, Elfira ran forward, emotion spilling from her like a tide. She threw her arms around Saphira, pressing close, her head tucked beneath Saphira's chin. Her whole body shook with the grief and love she could no longer contain.

Saphira wrapped her arms around her in return, holding her close.

Two sisters, from different worlds, bound by something deeper than time.

Neither of them spoke, for words were not needed.

Alfonso stepped forward with gentle solemnity, resting a steady hand on Saphira's shoulder. A moment later, Eleonora moved to her side, her presence calm and reassuring.

Elfira slipped one hand into Saphira's and held it tightly, her fingers refusing to let go, as if the very act of walking away might tear something precious from her heart.

Together, they began to move.

The crowd parted in silence, creating a path up the marble steps of the Grand Library.

The final light of evening caught on the silver of Saphira's cloak, casting a soft shimmer across the stone.

Behind them, Marek and Petrin followed at a respectful distance, their expressions composed, their footsteps measured. They were guardians to the very end.

The crowd stood in reverent stillness, their eyes following until the great doors closed behind her.

Down below, the elder scribe, Thalen, stepped forward to where Saphira had stood only moments before. He raised one hand gently and the square quietened once more.

'She has gone,' he said, 'but not from us.
What she has given will live in every heart that heard it.'

He looked to his fellow scribes, who nodded solemnly.

'We have recorded every word spoken this evening: every answer, every blessing. The Wisdom of Aloharin will be bound and preserved, for us and for those who come after.
A gift to this city. To the world.'

Applause rose again, this time accompanied by smiles and the quiet joy of something sacred entrusted to memory.

Back inside the library, the marble floors gleamed beneath the hush of dusk. The golden light had faded now, leaving only the quiet glow of the library lanterns and the faint shimmer of polished stone.

Saphira stood before the door to the Chamber of Wisdom.

Tears still clung to her cheeks. Her heart was beating fast, each breath soft and uneven in her throat.

She turned first to the Elders.

Alfonso stepped forward and embraced her, his usual calm broken by the weight of parting.

'Thank you,' he said, his voice thick with feeling. 'For everything.'

Eleonora's embrace followed, wordless, steady, filled with warmth and pride that needed no explanation, for it had all been said before.

Then Elfira flung her arms around Saphira once more, holding her tight and trembling, not yet ready to let go.

Saphira smiled through her tears, brushing a hand down Elfira's back.

'You will do beautifully,' she whispered. 'I know you will.'

At last, she turned to Marek and Petrin. The two men straightened as she approached, just as they had done every morning for seven years, quiet pillars of protection and trust.

She stepped into Marek's arms first.

'Thank you,' she said softly. 'You always made me feel safe.'

He bowed his head, his silver-streaked hair catching the last of the library's glow.

'It was my honour,' he replied, his voice low with reverence.

Then she turned to Petrin. His eyes shimmered and the quiet smile he always wore had softened with emotion.

'We'll miss you,' he said gently.

'And I will carry you both with me,' she answered, placing her hand briefly over her heart.

Then she turned to the door.

The stone glowed with a soft sapphire light, pulsing gently,

as though it had sensed her presence and was ready.

She reached out and pushed the door open with quiet care. Before stepping through, she turned for one final look: at those she had loved so completely, at the life that had changed her in every way.

Then she crossed the threshold.

The chamber welcomed her in a wash of golden light. Above her, the domed ceiling shimmered. The velvet sofa stood quietly by the wall, and beneath her feet, the inlaid floor curved in delicate, familiar patterns.

But it was the door at the far end that her eyes were drawn to. It was the one that had remained closed since the day she arrived.

And now, just as the door behind her clicked softly shut, that distant door creaked slowly open.

She stood still for a moment.

Then, slowly, she reached up and unclasped the silver cloak from her shoulders.

Beneath it, she wore garments that echoed those she had worn on the day she arrived. Familiar, yet subtly transformed. The fabrics were finer now, the cut more elegant, as though Arena, her seamstress and dear friend, had woven a memory into something new. A quiet fusion of two worlds: the one she had left behind and the one that had shaped her.

As the cloak slipped from her shoulders and pooled softly at her feet, Saphira ran a hand down her arm. Her fingers moved gently over the fabric and a wave of emotion rose within her.

Arena had given her more than clothing. She had given her a gift: a way to carry a piece of Aloharin with her. A thread of beauty and belonging to take back with her.

Saphira closed her eyes for a moment. She remembered the young woman she had been when she first stood in this chamber. The ache in her chest and the questions in her heart.

What am I even doing?

Will I ever feel happy?

What's the point?

Who am I meant to become?

And now... she knew.

She had answered each of those questions and more. She had walked through doubt, experienced deep joy, and had been transformed. She had poured herself into this life with everything she had to give, and in return, she had been changed.

She was no longer searching for her purpose.
She was living it.

She opened her eyes and took a slow, steady breath. One final breath of this sacred place.

Then she turned towards the open doorway. And with a heart full of everything she had become, she stepped forward into the world she once called home.

16

A New Beginning

Saphira stepped through the doorway and the light shifted. Gone was the gleam of marble and gold. Gone were the high domes and alcoves of gleaming books. She found herself standing on the old wooden floor of a quiet bookshop, sunlight slanting through the old windows onto the familiar spines of hardbacks and paperbacks stacked neatly on the oak shelves.

The scent of old paper and polished wood wrapped around her like an old friend, and in that quiet moment, she knew she was home.

She looked down at her clothes, her hands, her feet touching the wood. A part of her had half-expected to feel strange, as if waking from a dream. But she didn't. The shop was exactly as she remembered. The air was the same. And yet, she was not.

She ran her hand along the nearest shelf. The surface was cool beneath her fingertips, and a flood of memories filled her mind. First, she was reminded of her last visit to the bookshop, and then, with an overwhelming rush, came thoughts of her family and friends she had not seen for so long. Her eyes filled with tears, a love too big to contain.

The tears spilled over and she reached instinctively to wipe her face with her sleeve, but something in her pocket stopped her.

Her fingers touched soft fabric and she drew it out slowly. It was a handkerchief, white and finely stitched along its edges. In the corner, embroidered in the most beautiful blue silk, was an ornate letter S. And beneath it, in smaller letters, it read: *Love always, A*.

Another gift from Arena. So thoughtful and perfect, it brought more tears.

She held the handkerchief to her heart. Arena had known there would be tears, and so she had made this for her and tucked it into the pocket of the farewell clothes.

Sophia composed herself and used the handkerchief to dab her eyes gently. She stepped further into the shop, her eyes drifting across the shelves and windows, each detail stirring something distant and yet deeply familiar.

In the quiet, her thoughts returned to something she had often wondered about in the final days of her time in Aloharin. The prophecy had spoken of a return to her old world in which no time had passed. But what if it hadn't been true? What if seven years had passed here too?

The thought gave her a flutter of uncertainty. But then she remembered what she had come to trust with all her heart: the universe was always on her side. Whatever she found, it would be all right. She was exactly where she was meant to be.

Then she saw it.

Across the room, on the little round table near the window, sat a mug of hot chocolate and her books, just as she had left them. Her bag still hung on the back of the chair.

Relief and wonder bloomed in her chest. The prophecy had been true: seven years of beauty, wisdom, and love, yet not a single moment had passed here.

She took a few steps forward, emerging slowly from behind one of the tall bookshelves.

From behind the counter, Mrs Evelyn looked up.

She was just as Sophia remembered. Her grey hair was pinned neatly, and she was polishing her glasses with the hem of her cardigan. Her eyes, always so quietly perceptive, lingered on Sophia for a moment longer than usual.

Sophia was still dabbing her eyes with the handkerchief.

Mrs Evelyn paused, then asked gently, 'Sophia, my dear... are you quite all right?'

Sophia gave a small laugh and nodded.
'Oh yes. I just read something, and you know me – I get moved to tears so easily.'

Mrs Evelyn smiled knowingly.

'Oh, I know what you mean. Me too, dear.'

She paused again, then asked with quiet kindness,

'Did you find what you were looking for?'

Mrs Evelyn's question stirred something deep within her. A tide of memory and feeling rose in her chest. In that instant, she felt embraced by the beauty and wonder of Aloharin once again, and the quiet certainty that she had truly found what she was looking for.

Then she looked at Mrs Evelyn and smiled.

'Yes I did, thank you.'

Mrs Evelyn watched her for a moment, curiosity flickering behind her glasses. There was something different about Sophia, something lighter. Perhaps it was her clothes or something else, but she couldn't say exactly what.

Sophia returned to her table and gathered her things. She lifted her bag from the chair and reached for the books still spread across the table.

'Don't worry about the books, dear,' said Mrs Evelyn kindly. 'I'll put those back.'

Sophia smiled. 'Thank you.'

She offered a final smile, then walked to the door and pulled it gently open.

Outside, the sky was its usual soft grey. The village clock chimed the hour. Old Mr Cartwright pedalled slowly by, his familiar grin lighting up his face. Sophia couldn't help but smile.

It wasn't the gleaming white stone of Aloharin.

But it was beautiful.

The buildings. The bricks. The crooked signs swinging gently in the breeze. It was all so wonderfully ordinary.

A breeze brushed her face. The scent of damp earth and roses filled her lungs. She stood still, breathing it in, letting the ordinary beauty of the moment settle around her.

She thought of Aloharin. The people, the beautiful buildings, the laughter, the voices that would live in her forever. She missed them already. She knew in time the sorrow would ease, but the happy memories would remain in her heart always.

She looked down the quiet street ahead. The familiar cobblestones stretched before her, winding past the bakery, the old post office, the houses with their flower boxes and peeling paint. How many times had she walked this path, never seeing the beauty as she did now.

Now, every stone, every window, every passing face felt luminous. Not because they had changed, but because she had.

As she passed beneath the streetlamp outside the shop, it flickered gently to life. She paused and smiled, enjoying the quiet synchronicity. It was a gentle reminder of all she now knew: the beauty behind the ordinary, the unseen threads that connect all things, and the quiet magic that had always been there, waiting to be felt.

As she stepped over the cobbles, joy stirred in her chest. The world around her felt rich with meaning and gentle wonder. There was a lightness in her step, a sense of ease, as though life itself were walking beside her.

She knew there would still be challenges, still be moments of doubt or sorrow. But she was no longer afraid. She trusted the path ahead. She trusted herself. And she knew, with all her heart, that life would guide her, just as it always had.

She smiled again, enjoying who she had become.

Then she walked on, the cobbled street unfolding gently before her. A life waiting to be lived. A world waiting to be loved. And she, at last, was ready for it all.

Printed in Dunstable, United Kingdom